DIGITAL CAREER BUILDING™

CAREER BUILDING THROUGH

MACHINIMA

USING VIDEO GAMES TO MAKE MOVIES

HOLLY CEFREY

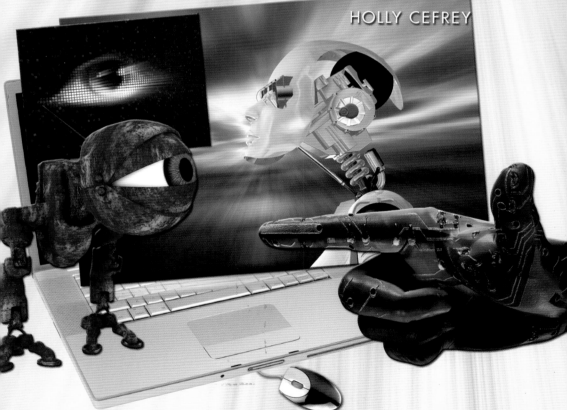

ROSEN
PUBLISHING®
New York

To my editor, Nick, and the Rosen gang. Your contribution to the world of books is inspiring!

Published in 2008 by The Rosen Publishing Group, Inc.
29 East 21st Street, New York, NY 10010

Library of Congress Cataloging-in-Publication Data

Cefrey, Holly.
Career building through machinima : using video games to make movies/Holly Cefrey. — 1st ed.
    p. cm. — (Digital career building)
Includes bibliographical references.
ISBN-13: 978-1-4042-1358-6 (library binding)
1. Digital cinematography—Vocational guidance—United States.
2. Computer games—Programming—Vocational guidance—United States.
3. Video games—Vocational guidance—United States. I. Title.
TR860.C45 2008
778.5'3023—dc22
                                                    2007028041

Manufactured in the China

CONTENTS

CHAPTER ONE
MACHINIMA MADNESS: A NEW ART FORM

Video gaming is a popular pastime in our global culture today. We love gaming so much that we can do it on our cell phones, other handheld devices, and home gaming or computer systems. We even can use the Web to play video games with people in other countries. According to the *International Journal of Computer Game Research*, more than $10 billion is spent around the world each year on video games.

Video games are popular because they appeal to our desire to play. Play is an open activity, oftentimes without rule and limits. It is an activity that is separate from our responsibilities and pressures. Video games allow us to take a break from the real world and all its

Video game culture and technology is embraced and celebrated at the 2006 E3 Video Game Expo.

stresses. Video gaming appeals to all ages, from young children to retirees or seniors. According to Matt Slagle of the Associated Press, 4 in 10 adults play video games on a regular basis.

Video games are the basis of a new art form known as machinima. Machinima is a combination of the words "machine" and "cinema." It is pronounced mah-sheen-eh-mah. Machinima describes what some incredibly creative people did with video games, starting in the 1990s. They decided to make movies by using video games. The people who make machinima are known as machinimists or machinimators.

Within a traditional film, there are many elements, such as backgrounds, scenes, and characters or actors. There are also artistic filming decisions, like whether the lighting of a scene will be dark or light. The director must make decisions about camera angles and shots. These elements already exist within a video game. The machinimist uses these elements to make a new story altogether. He or she may make modifications or changes to the elements such as altering the color of a character's clothing. Machinima is made entirely on a computer. There is no need for traditional film equipment, sets, and scenery.

The machinimist records a series of scenes and actions from the video game. Scenes may be edited together using editing software. Software is a program or set of instructions that tells a computer what to do. Once all of the scenes are recorded, new sound effects, voices, and music are added. Machinima may have very little to do with the original game itself. For example, a video game used for combat may be transformed into a funny film about two soldiers having an argument over what to eat for lunch.

Graphics, Sounds, Action!

The graphics, sounds, and themes in video games have evolved greatly over the years. Graphics are visual elements. An example of an early video game is *PONG* by Atari. A company like Atari that makes gaming software and consoles, or systems, is called a developer. *PONG* was a simple game that simulated, or imitated, a game of table tennis. The video game was in black and white, with two paddles. A small pong ball was hit back and forth between the players' paddles. The paddles could only move up or down on the screen. This incredibly simple game kept early gamers occupied for hours.

The graphics in *PONG* are an example of those that only had two dimensions. The paddles were rectangles with height and width. Something with height and width has two dimensions. The paddles were flat. They did not have volume or depth. Adding volume and depth makes graphics three dimensional. It is the difference between looking at a pillowcase and a pillow. The pillowcase is a rectangle that is flat. A pillow is a rectangle, too, but it also has volume and depth. The pillowcase is two dimensional, or 2-D. The pillow is three dimensional, or 3-D.

As game engine technology improved, so did game graphics. A game engine is what makes the game run. It processes the graphics, sounds, and actions of a game. In the 1990s, a company called id Software developed three games: *Wolfenstein 3-D*, *DOOM*, and *Quake*. The release

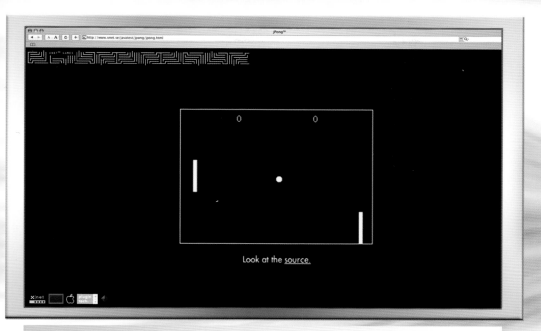

These are the bleak, flat graphics of *PONG*. *PONG* was one of the first home arcade games. It was created by Nolan Bushnell, who founded Atari in 1972.

of these games showed the true possibilities of game graphics. Objects with depth made the game and its environment seem more real.

The Birth of a Video Game

It can take years to develop a game, and many people make up a development team. The team includes computer programmers, writers, sound engineers, artists, and designers. Together, these people develop games, which are computer programs. These programs are made with lines of code. Code is a line of instruction. These instructions include how things will look, move, and sound in the game.

Joseph Saulter, chief executive officer of EAR, or Entertainment Arts Research, works on characters for a video game. Three-D software applications allow for modeling, animation, and other visual effects.

Designers decide the overall concept, or idea, of the game. They decide how it will look and feel. They decide the game's purpose and rules.

Artists make examples of the designer's ideas. 2-D artists do sketches. 3-D artists make three-dimensional models of the ideas. Background artists create the environment of the video game, like buildings or streets.

Sound engineers create the soundtrack of the game. They make scores and effects. Scores are the musical melodies. Effects are the sounds that you hear during a game, like a gunshot or screams.

Writers help pull all of the ideas together to produce scripts. The team uses scripts for direction on any particular element. Writers also create the game's manual and other technical communications.

Computer programmers write the code that becomes the game. For each game, there can be hundreds of thousands of lines of code. Engine programmers design the software that will make the game run. Graphic programmers work with the artists to make the designer's ideas come to life.

Another important role is the tester. The tester plays the game, looking for glitches. Information about the glitches is sent back to members of the development team so they can fix them. A game can be reprogrammed and retested several times before it finally reaches stores.

Modifications

The lines of code, graphics, themes, and ideas of a video game are property. Property is something that is owned. A game is the property of the software developer that created it. Thousands of dollars are spent to make a video game, and millions of dollars can be made from its sale. Companies protect their property. Laws are made to protect this property, too. When one developer "borrows" ideas, code, or themes from another game without permission, he or she can be sued by the owner.

The code of a video game usually is kept secret and is unavailable to the public. The makers of *DOOM* decided to share their code with the public in 1997. This code, also known as source code, was made available over the Web. Programmers and savvy gamers were encouraged to modify the game's code. By modifying or changing the code, they could change features in the game. These changes are known as "mods" (short for "modifications"). Fans also were allowed to share these mods. Id Software allowed this as long as fans did not charge each other to use the mods. The company wanted it to be a free exchange of ideas and code.

This was an incredible change for the gaming world. It allowed gaming enthusiasts to better understand game development and coding. Being able to manipulate the game environment is a big part of machinima.

TECH TOOLS Visit DevMaster.net to learn more about graphic engines and game engines. It is an organization that seeks to make deciding between the hundreds of game engines easier, based on user reviews, your needs, and other information.

Recording *Quake*: Let's Make a Movie!

When *Quake* was introduced in the mid-1990s, it took the gaming field by storm. The graphics were so enhanced

```
000                                    Game_local.cpp
// Copyright (C) 2004 Id Software, Inc.
//

#include "../idlib/precompiled.h"
#pragma hdrstop

#include "Game_local.h"

#ifdef GAME_DLL

idSys *                              sys = NULL;
idCommon *                           common = NULL;
idCmdSystem *                        cmdSystem = NULL;
idCVarSystem *                       cvarSystem = NULL;
idFileSystem *                       fileSystem = NULL;
idNetworkSystem *                    networkSystem = NULL;
idRenderSystem *                     renderSystem = NULL;
idSoundSystem *                      soundSystem = NULL;
idRenderModelManager *       renderModelManager = NULL;
idUserInterfaceManager *     uiManager = NULL;
idDeclManager *                      declManager = NULL;
idAASFileManager *                   AASFileManager = NULL;
idCollisionModelManager *    collisionModelManager = NULL;
idCVar *                             idCVar::staticVars = NULL;

idCVar com_forceGenericSIMD( "com_forceGenericSIMD", "0", CVAR_BOOL|CVAR_SYSTEM, "force generic platform independent SIMD" );

#endif

idRenderWorld *                      gameRenderWorld = NULL;    // all drawing is done to this world
idSoundWorld *                       gameSoundWorld = NULL;     // all audio goes to this world

static gameExport_t                  gameExport;

// global animation lib
idAnimManager                        animationLib;

// the rest of the engine will only reference the "game" variable, while all local aspects stay hidden
idGameLocal                          gameLocal;
idGame *                             game = &gameLocal;    // statically pointed at an idGameLocal

const char *idGameLocal::sufaceTypeNames[ MAX_SURFACE_TYPES ] = {
    "none", "metal", "stone", "flesh", "wood", "cardboard", "liquid", "glass", "plastic",
    "ricochet", "surftype10", "surftype11", "surftype12", "surftype13", "surftype14", "surftype15"
};

/*
===========
GetGameAPI
===========
*/
```

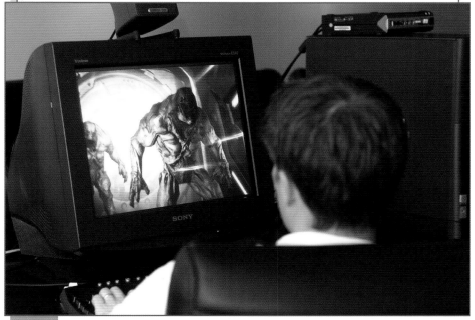

 The graphics on your screen are front side; code is the back side. Everything you see is produced through computer programming language or code.

that a player actually could look around his or her virtual environment. He or she could look left and see one perspective or view, then look right and see another. The characters in *Quake* also were able to move in realistic ways.

According to *BusinessWeek*, the earliest machinima projects were made in the mid-1990s. *Quake* was one of the first games to be used by machinimists. *Quake*, like *DOOM*, had another feature that gamers—and soon machinimists—loved. Gamers could record a game and play it back later. This is known as game play recording. This allowed a gamer to show off his or her unique skills to viewers. *Quake* gamers formed groups to compete in and display their recorded games, also called demos. "Demos" is short for "demonstrations." The games were recorded and then played back.

WATCH OUT If you find a machinima Web site or interest group that wants to charge you money for posting or viewing projects, you should consider free Web sites first. Two of the most popular free sites are Machinima.com and Machinima.org.

One gaming group was called the Rangers. In 1996, it recorded a demo that became a machinima. It was just over a minute and a half long. The dialogue, or the words characters speak, is texted across the top of the screen, rather than actually spoken. A soldier is camped in one place, hoping to have the action come to him instead of seeking out battle. A few team members are looking for the camped soldier. Two rangers go out to

MACHINIMA MADNESS: A NEW ART FORM

 John Romero (*center, light shirt*) and other industry innovators: (*left to right*) David Najjab, Richard Gray, Paul Jaquays, Tom Hall, and Peter Raad. They developed a program in electronic gaming that is now offered as an accredited master's degree through the Guildhall at SMU.

scout, and the camper kills them. The remaining rangers shoot the camper and kill him. As they stand over his remains, the rangers identify the camper as an enemy named John Romero.

 View this historical machinima that started an art form at http://www.machinima.com/films.php?id = 31.

In the real world, John Romero is a well-known game programmer, developer, and designer. He is a cofounder of id Software, the company behind *Quake*.

Ironic humor like this—killing a well-known game developer (in the virtual world)—is a hallmark, or major element, of machinima. The Rangers' demo is titled *Diary of a Camper*. It generally is credited as being the first machinima, although back then it was called *Quake Movie*. The noun "machinima" was introduced around 2000 to describe movies made from video games.

CHAPTER TWO

3-D IN THE REAL WORLD

The brilliance of using a video game to produce a film means that anyone who owns a game system could be a film producer. Therefore, machinima has a democratizing effect. When something is democratic, it means that everyone has equal access to it. Global Web sites such as YouTube and Machinima.com showcase machinima for the masses. All you have to do is post it, free of charge. Everyone else can view it, free of charge. What this means is that veteran game developers and newbie game players alike can submit films in the same venue or place. It would be like a new film student having his or her first attempt at filmmaking showcased next to a Steven Spielberg film.

Video-sharing sites, such as YouTube, provide an excellent and easy way to collect, share, and review film projects from all over the world.

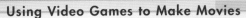

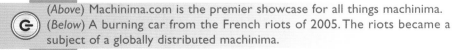

(*Above*) Machinima.com is the premier showcase for all things machinima.
(*Below*) A burning car from the French riots of 2005. The riots became a
subject of a globally distributed machinima.

Making People Pay Attention

According to the BBC, two French teenagers were electrocuted—or shocked to death—when they climbed into a power substation on October 27, 2005. This occurred in a suburb of Paris called Clichy-sous-Bois. Claims were made that the youths were trying to escape from police. Officials have declared that the police were not chasing the teens, thus they did not cause the deaths. Either way, the event triggered rioting throughout Paris and its suburbs. According to the *Washington Post*, more than 10,000 automobiles were torched. More than 500 buildings were damaged. The rioting lasted throughout October and November.

It was widely reported that the rioting occurred in poor areas where many African Muslim immigrant families live. This is a population, according to CNN, that totals more than 5 million people. Many in the population had expressed their unhappiness prior to the teens' deaths. They were discriminated against, denied jobs, and denied a secure living.

A twenty-seven-year-old industrial designer named Alex Chan decided to make a machinima about the riots. His screen name is Koulamata. Chan used the game engine from *The Movies*, which was developed by Lionhead Studios. According to BusinessWeek, his project took less than a week to produce. The film is titled *The French Democracy*, and it lasts just over thirteen minutes.

The film opens with a scene of two youths entering a power station after being chased. Once their deaths are announced, the film follows the struggles of other French characters. One is denied a job. He also is denied a place to live. Another is put in jail overnight because he forgot his passport, even though he is a natural citizen. Another is beaten by police in an alleyway. The young men decide that they cannot stand it any longer. They band together and riot. The English subtitles remind viewers that France was once a land known for its freedom, equality, and fraternity. The characters in Alex Chan's film were denied the benefits of these three values.

Chan Goes Global

Chan merely posted his film on Lionhead Studio's Web site. The company encourages the use of *The Movies* for machinima. The game is about film producers who create their own movies, sets, and characters. As a player, you are the mogul or executive creating your own film. According to *BusinessWeek*, one new machinima is posted on Lionhead's Web site every minute.

 See Alex Chan's *The French Democracy* at *The Movies* Web site http://movies.lionhead. com/movie/11520. Chan released a second machinima called Seeds of Terrorism in 2006. It was produced by Bac Films.

Chan's project gained immediate attention. It was distributed to MTV, YouTube, and machinima sites such as Machinima.com. More than 42,000 viewers have watched the film at Machinima.com. Newspapers including the *Washington Post* have highlighted Chan's project as a new way to reach the masses.

Paul Marino, executive director of the Academy of Machinima Arts & Sciences and author of *The Art of Machinima*, posted comments about the film on his public blog. "While I'm not sure machinima can or will propagate political rights activism across borders or cultures," he wrote, "the medium does provide the power to do so."

For Free or For Sale

The French Democracy is an example of commercial and noncommercial use. A commercial project means that it is used or meant to make a profit for its creators. Noncommercial means the opposite. It is created for reasons other than making a profit. Alex Chan's noncommercial film was made from a commercial game by Lionhead Studios. Lionhead allows gamers to freely use its game for noncommercial use.

When a gamer uses *The Movies* to make a movie, Lionhead encourages the gamer to post the movie at its Web site. As the purchaser of the game, you own the movie that you make with it. It is your property, according to Lionhead. You do not own the assets, however. Assets are the elements of the game, like the characters and scenes. Assets also can mean the code, themes, character names, stories, dialogues, animation, sounds, music, and effects. Since you do not own the assets, you are not allowed to make any money off of the sale of any movie made with *The Movies*. You are its author, but not the game's author. Chan is not allowed to sell his film, but he is allowed to distribute it. Should he decide to make money off of it, he would have to negotiate with Lionhead.

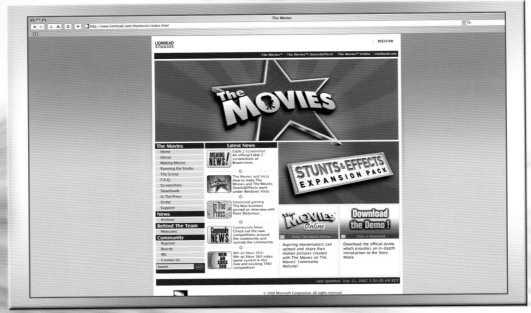

At *The Movies* Web site, you can watch other fans' movies and read up on great tips and tricks. You can upload your own homemade movies from *The Movies* game.

In many cases, the developer would negotiate an agreement that would allow use of the assets for a fee. The machinimist would pay a fee to be able to use the assets to make a profit. This is called a license agreement.

WATCH OUT Commercial games have agreements, often called End User License Agreements, which tell you what you can and cannot do with the property. You are the end user and are expected to agree to the terms in order to use the game. If the agreement does not mention rules for machinima, you can send an e-mail to the developer asking for permission.

Gaming companies often generously enter into agreements with machinimists when a project becomes popular. An example is the *Red vs. Blue: The Blood Gulch Chronicles* series, which began in 2003. Machinima actually brings attention to the game from which it is based. Viewers see a film they like, and then they buy the game in order to play the game or produce their own film. *Red vs. Blue* brought the game *Halo* to the general public's attention.

Red vs. Blue: The Blood Gulch Chronicles

Red vs. Blue is a famous machinima series based on the games *Halo* and *Halo 2*. *Halo* is a game environment where you and your friends can battle aliens in a vast terrain of bunkers, bases, and the outdoors. The creators of *Red vs. Blue*, however, made an entirely different plot for *Halo's* assets.

The series began in 2003, with episodes that average between two and five minutes. Michael Burns (also known as Bernie) and a few friends loved playing *Halo*. They played the game together, by hooking their Xbox game consoles to the Internet, and signed on to a single game. Doing so allowed them to play against each other, rather than fighting aliens. Any cool tricks that they created were recorded. Burns posted the recordings on a gaming Web site to show others how to do the tricks.

Just for fun, Burns recorded some voiceovers for a demo, making the soldier's thoughts and words known to the viewer. This was just as exciting as recording tricks. He and his friends wrote a script, recorded voices, and acted out scenes using the game. They recorded and posted the film. According to the *New York Times*, 20,000 people viewed the film in one day. Burns and his friends

The amazing and engaging graphics of the *Halo* game series make a budding director's work exciting, as well as the veteran filmmakers of Rooster Teeth Productions (*Red vs. Blue*).

eventually formed Rooster Teeth Productions, a machinima production company.

Bungie Studios is a subsidiary of the computer giant, Microsoft. The team at Bungie decided to support the *Red vs. Blue* series, since the popularity of the series allowed people outside of gaming to learn about *Halo*.

Four Years of Webisodes

The running plot of *Red vs. Blue* is that two teams of soldiers are in combat with each other, but there is very little combat at all. Instead of gunplay, each episode shows us clever dialogue and interaction between team members and enemies. The aliens from the original *Halo* game have minor parts, rather than being the menacing enemy. One of the characters has an alien as his child. A tank was given a computer personality and she has a mind and motivations of her own, much to the annoyance of her team. The humor of Rooster Teeth's team, combined with the dynamic graphics of Bungie Studios, quickly created a cult and commercial classic.

The team stayed on a tight schedule, producing episodes on a weekly basis. According to the *New York Times*, almost one million people were watching a new episode every Friday. The series can be viewed at the company's Web site, RoosterTeeth.com. Continuing stories or series on the Web are known as webisodes. The series was so popular that the public begged for the episodes to be sold on DVD. This would involve the legal issues of using someone else's property for commercial use.

Microsoft gave Rooster Teeth permission to use the game without paying any licensing fees. Microsoft also hired Rooster Teeth to produce promos or commercials for their *Halo* game series using the *Red vs. Blue* characters. Microsoft even went so far as to upgrade *Halo* with machinimists in mind. A newer version of *Halo* lets characters lower their weapons. This makes it easier for dialogue scenes in machinima.

CHAPTER THREE

TOOLS OF THE TRADE

Because machinima is new, many of the projects you see are pioneering efforts. Game developers are just now beginning to add machinima-friendly features to standard games. Otherwise, machinima has been an ad-hoc activity. This means gamers and programmers strung together various techniques and tools to produce machinima. Early machinima projects showcase the creativity of gamers, but also their coding and programming abilities. Early machinima was produced by fans who knew how to manipulate code, a game system, computer programs, or computer networks, at the very least.

Because *The Movies* is about making movies, a gamer is able to produce movies from within the game.

Two players engage in gameplay on their PC, or personal computer.

The French Democracy was Alex Chan's first try at making a film, and it ended up circling the globe. According to *BusinessWeek*, Chan was neither a gamer nor a filmmaker before this project. Anyone—with any level of experience—is just one project away from making machinima, depending on the tools that you use.

Your first step would be to decide what story you would like to tell. You will need to choose a game engine. *Red vs. Blue* shows that even though the characters are soldiers, the film does not have to be about combat. Once you decide your story, you'll want to build a list of characters. Ask yourself: Who will be in the film? What motivates each character or actor? Then you can consider other elements such as scenes, mood, and audio or sound. Ultimately, you will want to pull all of these elements together in a script. The script will help you organize your story, characters, scenes, dialogue, and ideas.

Machinima-Oriented Games

There are a few games that already have machinima tools built in. As mentioned, *The Movies* lets you record any number of scenes. The time period for the game spans from about 1920 to 2005. There are more than forty sets to choose from as backdrops for your film. In Story or Sandbox modes, you can make any kind of movie you desire. It can be an action film, romance, sci-fi, or comedy. The game only is available on Windows, but a Mac version is in the works.

Most 3-D games of this nature may require that your computer have expanded capabilities. These include

Real Player (http://www.real.com) and Windows Media Player allow computer users to view machinima if the film is saved as a WMP file.

3-D Hardware Accelerator Cards. Video and 3-D cards allow for detailed graphic display. They boost the performance of your computer system. Graphic files use a lot of memory and require a lot of processing. Accelerator cards take that load off of your main processing unit.

WATCH OUT When buying games for computers, make sure you read the requirements. If you don't have some of the elements, you'll need to buy them. Begin a list of what you'll need and research prices. This will help you decide whether the expense is affordable or worth it.

To take a film from gaming applications to viewing it across systems requires rendering. When you render something, you transfer it from one form to another. All of your core machinima files need to be capable of being played back or viewed. The most common video/movie players are RealPlayer, Windows Media Player, and QuickTime. Machinima from *The Movies* is rendered so that it plays on Windows Media Player (WMP). Mac users can still view WMP files if they install the WMP for Mac (various versions are available for free on the Web). The standard movie player for Mac is QuickTime. Once saved for the specific players, the files can be uploaded to the Web as well.

Another game with machinima tools is *Sims 2*. The *Sims* series are examples of sim games. "Sim" stands for "simulated." These games are designed to seem very lifelike. Life is unpredictable. Characters are programmed to act as you want them to, but they are programmed to do their own thing as well. When you use sim games for

 Wall-to-wall simulation scenes feature video game characters interacting with one another. Such characters have become the virtual actors for machinima.

machinima, the results are not always predictable. You may want two characters to talk in a scene, but if they do not like each other, they may ignore each other. A character may get tired in the middle of a scene, rather than do as you wish. She or he may decide to go take a nap!

Shooting desired scenes in sim games can take hours of preparation. You may have to expose two characters to each other several times before they decide to talk to each other. This challenge is exciting for machinimists. They must figure out how to motivate their "actors" to do as directed.

Unreal Tournament 2004 also has tools that allow for machinima projects. Unreal Editor lets you create new levels and character skins. The skin is the exterior of a

3-D character. You can customize elements such as color. You can record and edit sequences to produce films using the Matinee tool. Other games with machinima features include *Halo 2*, *Doom 3*, *Battlefield 1942*, *Battlefield 2*, *Half-Life 2*, and *World of Warcraft*, and sport series such as *FIFA*, *NHL*, and *NFL*.

In Addition to Quake or DOOM

Machinimation is a program made by Fountainhead Entertainment. You use a version with either *Quake* or *DOOM* engines. It was designed to deliver more machinima tools to both games. It allows you to do studio-like things, like set up more than one camera angle per scene. You can script the actions of the characters, rather than relying on game play.

A CLOSER LOOK Take a look at Katherine Anna Kang's *Anna*. Kang is the president of Fountainhead Entertainment. Her company's product, *Machinimation*, was used to make *Anna* on the *Quake* engine. It won the Best Technical Achievement award at the Machinima Film Festival in 2003.

Separate Recording Software

There are applications such as *Fraps*, *Gamecam*, and *FastCap* that record your games. These applications are known as video and/or audio capture programs. They are designed to "capture" a feed of data, whether it is a game, film, or sound file. They record in real time, while you're playing a game (or acting out a scene). Once the video is captured, you're ready to begin editing.

 Fraps (http://www.fraps.com) is a video capturing software application that allows Windows users to capture their video game scenes to produce machinima.

Your Production Team, Based on a Leader

Rooster Teeth, which produces *Red vs. Blue*, is a fully dedicated machinima company. The organization's Web site has a forum where members can ask any question, even a technical one. The team shared their tricks of the trade with *Computer Graphics World* in 2005.

The team first makes a script. They record the dialogue on their computer by using Adobe's *Audition*. This application makes it possible for the team to record and mix sounds. Once they have the audio track, they are ready for visuals.

Games systems such as Xbox open up a whole new world of great graphics and demo recording, which can be turned into machinima.

Each character you see in *Red vs. Blue* is like a puppet, with a gamer as its puppeteer. The scenes are provided by *Halo 2*. Rooster Teeth uses four Xbox consoles that are linked together so that up to twelve characters can interact in one scene. When systems are linked together, it is called a network. One of the Xboxes is directly linked to a computer. A character in one Xbox provides the perspective or view of what all the characters are doing in the linked game. A cameraman/puppeteer will move the character's head and position, which provides different camera angles. The viewed scenes are collected on a video capture card in the computer.

The video is edited in Adobe's *Premiere*. This is a video capture and editing program for Macs and Windows. It has an audio mixer. The team views the work on two large flat-panel monitors. Once the video and audio are combined, then the film is almost ready. They put a letterbox frame around the edges of the film. This frame gives the feel of a real movie and hides game information. Finally, the team saves the film in a variety of formats, like WMV or QuickTime. They then use Adobe's *Encore DVD* to format the series for DVD distribution.

Editing

Editing is the part where you'll bring all of your scenes together. You may decide that a scene it too long, so you'll shorten it. If you want to add a lot of features, you will want to use an editing tool that is powerful. Editing affects your storytelling. It is a skill in itself. Randall Glass, creator of the famous machinima *Warthog Jump: A Halo Physics Experiment*, sees machinima as a "great way to learn storytelling and editing."

The Overcast site (http://www.theovercast.com) is a blog and podcast listing of machinima projects and events around the world.

Warthog Jump was an experiment of various explosions set to songs. It begins with a line from *The Matrix*, stating, "Tank, Load the Jump Program." The project, just under three minutes and thirty seconds, shows a series of stunts done with a jeep, known as a warthog. Randall's character places grenades in specific locations, and then throws more grenades. The character sends jeep after jeep skyrocketing. He even takes his character for a ride through the sky, by jumping on the jeep as it blows. One jeep remains twirling in the air for more than eight seconds.

The film was edited on Mac's *iMovie* and released in QuickTime format. It set off a whole new theme for machinima, known as warthog jumping. Glass's *Warthog Jump* was nominated for Best Editing at the 2002 Machinima Festival.

 Watch the machinima that set off a global craze. *Halo* fans create experiments of their own in order to pay tribute (and try to top) *Warthog Jump* at Warthog-Jump.com.

Glass suggests that you visit theovercast.com which supplies detailed podcasts about machinima, as well as links for all levels of machinimists. He views *The Movies* as a great starter tool, which will enrich your story-telling and editing skills. *The Movies* comes with editing tools that allow you to change the order of your scenes, the lighting, weather, and mood.

CHAPTER FOUR

TURNING GAMING SKILLS INTO A CAREER

Machinimists are creative people. They take what they see and change it. They build what isn't there. They use things in new ways, different than the original intent or purpose. Even the process of using a game's limited or overloaded features can be difficult, requiring more creativity—and patience.

If you love a game, but it does not have recording or machinima features, you will need to invent a way to use it. Instead of connecting to a computer with capturing and editing programs, you might use a camcorder. You would need to research how to make this technique work. Search the Web for advice and instructions for your particular idea.

A graphic artist or designer begins a sketch of the background that will be used for a video game.

You must stretch your imagination and knowledge to create a system that works for you, with what you have and can afford. To develop your creativity, keep an open mind and be patient. Unless you have a deep understanding of computer science and information technology, not everything will be known to you. Even incredibly skilled programmers have dumbfounding moments. Fortunately, the online machinima community offers many free resources to help when you feel overwhelmed. If you have a complicated written manual in front of you, don't be discouraged. Join a gaming or machinima forum and ask questions about the things that you don't understand. You will find that the machinima community is very helpful.

TECH TOOLS There usually are free or demo versions of most software and plug-ins. Get free tools when you can, but only when they come from a trusted source. For free programming, Web site downloads, and help, check out FreeProgrammingResources.com and TheFreeCountry.com.

A great way to boost your creativity is to see what others are doing with the games you like. Watch machinimas that come from your favorite game. See what the creator is doing with the characters, sets, lighting, editing, and plot. Let his or her work inform you of the possibilities. Critique or think critically about the work: What is neat about it? What is wrong about it? What would make it better? These questions will help unlock your imagination.

Sites like FreeProgrammingResources.com can make a budding programmer's work much easier. They collect the world and technology of programming in one place for your education, for free.

Getting into Gaming

Many well-known machinimists will say that they love gaming. *Red vs. Blue* grew out of a love for *Halo*. Michael Burns told *Computer Graphics World*, "I still play it all the time." Maybe you have been told that you spend too much time gaming. If you think in terms of filmmaking, however, you will maximize this "downtime." You will be able to turn a hobby into a great form of expression. Perhaps machinima will allow you to say things that you cannot say in real life.

If you're not really into gaming, you should at least try to become familiar with the game you want to use.

As machinima becomes mainstream, seminars and workshops like the one above at mediamatic.net will happen near you. This one took place at Mediamatic in Amsterdam.

By playing the game, you will know what the characters are capable of as far as movement. You will want to understand timing and spacing within the game so that you can plan your scenes. There are also neat tricks within games, which are mostly discovered by skilled gamers. These tricks make for dramatic cinematic events when carried out properly.

Developing even minimal game skills will make your efforts in machinima easier. You should record a few demos and watch them to see how recorded graphics look within the game you chose. Write down any ideas you have, and play the game to see if you can make them happen.

Outside of knowing how to game, there are several other skills that are a part of machinima. Fortunately, many of them are transferable. Film, art, programming, and design all represent different and shared skill sets. They also represent fields in which there are hundreds of interesting careers. You would benefit from studying any of these fields so that you can supplement or help your machinima projects with a dependable income.

A Budding Film Career

Knowing about traditional film and developing film skills will help your machinima career because machinimas are film. In film, there is preproduction, production, and postproduction. The same is true for machinima. If you study film, you could apply many of its techniques in your machinima. Studying film will broaden your skill set as well. Have a backup plan in case you decide that machinima will merely be your hobby.

Studying film can strengthen your creativity for machinima. *Citizen Kane*, shown here, is considered one of the greatest films of all time.

When you study film, you don't just learn about equipment and techniques. You study the history and art of film. You learn to think critically about why certain films are successful and why others fail. You see how to convey or share ideas through a visual world. You learn how to tell a story through dialogue or lack of dialogue. You realize how music makes a film better, or worse. You also learn the business side of film that includes budgets and deadlines. All of this applies to machinima.

What areas of film truly interest you? Do you love thinking up stories and telling them to friends? Are you great at writing dialogue? Do you know exactly what actor would fit a role? Could you direct a whole production?

Do you think you would be great at making sure a big studio stays on budget? Would you love to take the director's work and edit it? Are you great with matching songs to moods?

While you may be doing all of the above for your machinima, perhaps a single area interests you the most. If so, you could expand your machinima team to include members who are better at the other skills. This way, you can focus on what you love to do and on being the best at it. By having others who are better at other things join you, you can benefit from their strengths.

Graphic Design and Art

Machinima is a visual medium. A medium is a means for communication. Machinima relies on great graphics to captivate its viewer. In your first machinima projects, you may just take the scenes and characters as they come. With mods, you can change these artistic elements. Doing so will allow you to recreate the environment and personalize it. Soon, you may find that you want to create whole new characters and environments.

All of the elements in a game that you see— characters, background, sets, levels, character animation, and sounds—are created by artists. Some of these artists have core art backgrounds. They know elements of shape, color, illustration, photography, painting, and computer-based design. Some have programming backgrounds. They know about art and design, but they also have a background in computer science.

There are several different disciplines within art. You begin by studying the basics of art, like history, style, colors, and realism. You learn how to work with different

Programming and Software Engineering

Your video game owes its existence to computer science and information technology. Within these disciplines, there are several roles. For game coding and software, there are programmers and software engineers. People tend to think these are the same role, but there is a difference.

Programmers are writers. They create and assemble code. Lines of code become instructions called programs. The programs tell computers and game systems what to do. Programmers test and debug code. There are different languages for programming. Languages include C ++, Java, and Prolog. Within each language, there can be more than one way to instruct a computer to do something. There can be pieces of code from other programs that can be reused. There can be new technologies just coming into play that could be used if developed just a little further. This is where the software engineer comes in.

A software engineer is like an editor. He or she makes specifications for the programmer to follow. In this case, it means a detailed plan. It explains the project, its purpose, and the amount of time that will be spent on it. It suggests what code should be written from scratch and which can be copied from other programs. The software engineer wants to make the program as close to what the client wants as possible. He or she will have had detailed conversations with the client. From that, technologies are assigned, budgets are formed, and deadlines are put in place.

You don't need to be a programmer to be a successful machinimist, but knowing code can't hurt. There may be one detail about your game that you would love to fix. A few lines of code could do the trick!

mediums such as paint, ink, pencil, and computer imaging. You discover to render what you see in life into 2-D and 3-D forms.

 For some of the most amazing digital art around, check out CGSociety.org. This is the CGS Society (Society of Digital Arts) Web site. It is a global organization dedicated to providing resources for digital artists.

Within the world of gaming artists, there are lead artists, character artists, character animators, and background artists. There are also technical artists, 2-D, 3-D, texture, and FX artists. What do you like to create? Do you like to take someone's ideas and produce drawings? Can you take someone's designs and animate them? Can you produce sound effects to go with actions? Examining what you really like to do can allow you to find a career in graphic and gaming arts, while getting your feet wet in machinima.

Video Game Designer

Perhaps you've already made several machinimas. You may have produced several far-out mods already because you're an excellent programmer. A machinist who can reprogram a game, reconstruct 3-D characters and environments, and swap technologies could have a career as a video game designer.

Imagine turning one of your machinimas into its own video game. A video game designer has all the tools to design and develop a video game. This designer has a background in both programming and art. You would study software engineering along with graphic design.

 A simple idea can turn into a global gaming hit. Shigeru Miyamoto created games like *Donkey Kong*, *Super Mario Brothers*, and the *Legend of Zelda*.

You would learn interactive programming and 2-D and 3-D modeling.

As game development is a science, there are many challenges. A core skill for any designer is problem-solving ability. You will learn how to empower yourself with resources when you encounter new problems. Since a game begins with a story, another key skill is story-telling. The game designer builds upon that story to produce characters and their environments.

CHAPTER FIVE

THE BEST OF BOTH WORLDS: SUCCESS IN THE DIGITAL ARTS

Would you feel successful if your machinima were featured on a popular Web site and viewed 40,000 times? What if you were hired by a dedicated machinima production studio and could support yourself? Would success merely mean completing your first machinima and moving on to something else? Careers in the arts are not always predictable, so you will need a flexible understanding of what success means. Your achievement in machinima will be what you make it.

If you're planning for a long-term career in machinima, seek to empower yourself with knowledge and training. Get to know the machinima community. Currently, there are only a handful of dedicated

A Web site can be published overnight and changed in a minute. Web and digital arts allow for customization for anyone with the skills.

machinima studios, so direct jobs may be hard to come by, depending on where you live. Start studying the various disciplines that machinima involves. Explore local resources such as community colleges and art schools. They may offer summer prep courses before you graduate from high school.

Organizations and Events

Sometimes, the best career advice comes from industry giants. They have been through various challenges. They have seen great success. If they are willing to share their knowledge, you stand to benefit. Because machinima is new, most of its stars are actively promoting the art form. They see it as a new method of communication that is practical and has endless possibilities.

So far, there is one major nonprofit organization known as the Academy of Machinima Arts & Sciences in New York. Its mission is to "promote, organize, and recognize the growth of machinima filmmaking and filmmakers." It formed in 2002 through the work of several machinima leaders. The current board members have been working in the medium since its beginnings. They include Hugh Hancock of Strange Company; Paul Marino and Frank Dellario of ILL Clan; and Friedrich Kirschner, who is an independent developer. Among previous board members was Katherine Anna Kang of Fountainhead Entertainment.

Community Contributors

Strange Company is a production studio fully dedicated to machinima. It produced *Ozymandias*, which was

 Jim Bannister, Burnie Burns, Paul Marino, and Matthew Ross introduced the topic of machinima to the 2005 Sundance Film Festival.

praised by famous movie critic Roger Ebert. Strange Company was founded by Hugh Hancock and Gordon McDonald. They are responsible for creating the leading machinima Web site, Machinima.com.

Since 2000, their Web site has published more than 3,000,000 pages and 300 articles. Strange Company sold the site in 2004. It has produced a full-length film, *BloodSpell*, based on the game *Neverwinter Nights*. It can be viewed at BloodSpell.com.

The company is based in Scotland. It posts ads for employees and volunteers. Checking this page regularly will inform you of the skills that a production company would be looking for. See StrangeCompany.org.

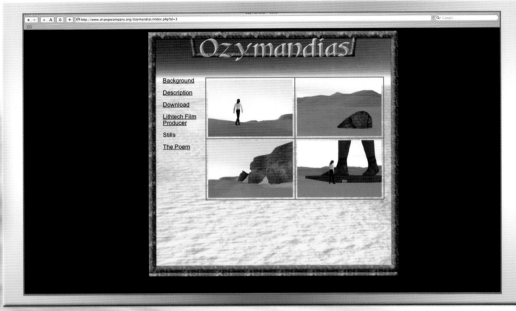

The Strange Company's Web site (http://www.strangecompany.org) offers free downloads of its film *Ozymandias*. *Ozymandias* was originally a poem written by Percy Shelley, husband of Mary Shelley, author of *Frankenstein*.

The ILL Clan is a fully dedicated machinima group based in Brooklyn, New York. It is made up of 3-D artists, filmmakers, and improvisational comedians. Improvisational means to be made up as it happens. While it produces projects for hire—clients include Audi—it's elevating the art form to new heights. The group has taken machinima to the theater, performing in front of a live audience. The characters interact on a screen as ILL Clan members provide the voices.

The ILL Clan, at ILLClan.com, is well known for its machinima hit *Apartment Hunting*. It was released in 1998 and is based on *Quake*. The plot follows two lumberjacks as they try to rent an apartment together.

 There are cool ways to connect with a community. Here, a student interested in a video game job watches a virtual job fair within the Second Life online game.

The company's corporate Web site, The Electric Sheep Company (an add-on software developer), lists job ads. Visit ElectricSheepCompany.com to get an idea of what requirements are needed for roles within the company.

The Academy of Machinima Arts & Sciences holds an annual awards show for the best machinimas in the industry. It is now being broadcast in *Second Life*, so if you have a character in the game, you can actually watch the awards show in the virtual realm. In 2006, the event was held at the Museum of the Moving Image in New York.

The awards are known as Mackies. A large panel of industry leaders reviews the nominated films and

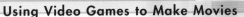
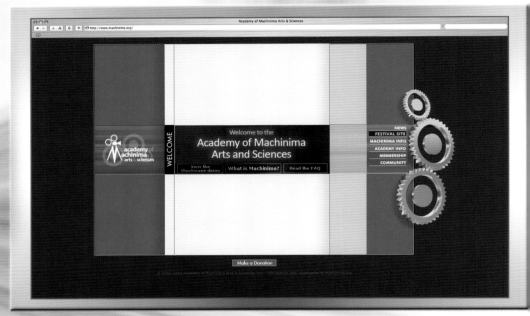

The Academy of Machinima Arts & Sciences Web site (http://www.machinima.org) will teach you about basics of machinima, as well as connect you with the larger machinima community.

gives awards for categories such as Best Editing, Best Directing, and Best Picture. Since 2002, the Mackie nominees and awardees represent some of the most innovative machinima to date. View your peer's work at www.machinima.org in the festival link.

You may find that there are machinimists such as Hugh Hancock speaking at digital media events. This is a great way to learn about the field and how to build a career in it. If you can't see industry leaders in person, research the Web for video clips of events. Most of these events are webcast or archived so that you can view them at any time. Checking the podcast http://theovercast.com will also provide you with an archive of events or links to more information.

Your Portfolio

As a digital arts pro, you will want to maximize certain areas in order to gain increased exposure. You can submit your machinima to sites such as YouTube or Machinima.com. If your game's developer supports machinima, it may have a posting site, too. Posting across all machinima sites will bring your work the most attention. Many of these sites require you to join as a member.

WATCH OUT There are rules of membership for most forums. Most machinima sites do not allow trolling or flaming. This means posting remarks in a forum that are likely to cause an argument. Make sure to read the rules before joining online machinima communities or organizations.

You can host your own site, showcasing your own work. This would be your digital version of a portfolio. Artists use portfolios to try to get work. The online version would include clips of your machinimas. Web sites are an inexpensive way of reaching future employers and clients. Hosting packages can cost $10 a month and up, depending on the features. With an online portfolio, you merely can give someone the URL or link. When visiting your site, that person will not only understand your abilities in machinima, but he or she also will get a sense of your professionalism.

Research various portfolios across the Web. Evaluate what makes a great online portfolio and what doesn't. Most surfers want a major element—ease of navigation. How easily can someone find information about you, your work, and your goals on your site? Another element is language. How are you expressing yourself on your Web site? Are you using professional communication, or are you speaking informally? Many sites offer a mixture of both, depending on the topic being covered.

Making a Go of Machinima

The machinima world is just beginning to grow. You'll find all kinds of artists and all levels of professionalism on the Web. Marketing techniques include using racy language to express a hot new release. Just because you see informal language being used doesn't mean that you have to imitate it. Writing skills are an essential part of machinima. Can you express and excite others by using the right words without getting racy? Challenge yourself to do so. You never know where your machinima may end up, and you want your descriptions to be usable in all forums.

If you join a production company at a junior level, you will face many challenges. Production companies work around deadlines. Hours may be very long as a deadline approaches. Keeping a positive attitude, even in a stressful environment, is the right thing to do. Allowing yourself to get caught up in the stress only adds to the problem. By remaining calm, you will be able to focus and assist wherever you are needed most. This is a valuable, professional quality that leaders take note of and admire. Dedicating yourself fully and professionally in the beginning stages of your career will allow you to advance more quickly.

 YouTube allows you to view countless videos, including machinima projects. Here, the posting for Zero 7's video/machinima of *In the Waiting Line.*

 Take a look at the first music video to use machinima. It was for Zero 7, produced by Fountainhead Entertainment and Ghost Robot. *In the Waiting Line* won three machinima awards in 2003 and introduced the music video world to a new medium.

As machinima becomes more mainstream, more resources will become available. For instance, Michigan State University introduced a class called Machinima (TC 448) to its core curriculum in 2006. It started as an independent study idea but blossomed into a new offering in the Telecommunication, Information Studies, and Media Department.

Getting in on machinima as it is still making its way is an exciting thing to do. You have more access to the stars of machinima, as they are actively promoting the medium and encouraging others to start. Someone such as Alex Chan can go from a simple idea to speaking at events, to newspapers, and producing a new project at an actual film production company. Are you the next Alex Chan?

GLOSSARY

ad-hoc Pulled together to serve a new purpose.

assets Elements of a game, like characters, sounds, and code.

code A line of instruction that tells a computer or application what to do.

console The hardware of a game system.

demo A recorded version of something for the use of demonstration.

democratize The ability to bring equality.

developer A company that builds software or systems.

game engine The core component of a system that process graphics and makes the game run.

graphics Visual elements of a game, like a character or background.

improvise Making something up as you go along.

license agreement A legal agreement where legal use of another person's or company's property is established.

medium Means for communication.

modifications (mods) Changes in the code of a game that allow for changes in visual elements, like characters and scenes.

navigation To move deliberately toward a location.

network When two or more computers are linked together.

program A set of instructions that tells a computer or system how to function.

render To transfer from one form to another.

score Musical melody or complete work.

script The written version of a movie or theatrical production.

simulate To make a very close imitation of the real thing.

skin The two-dimensional cover of a three-dimensional figure.

source code Core programming language that is translated into machine language for a program to run.

software Program or set of instructions that tells a computer or system what to do.

specifications Detailed plan with requirements and rules.

supplement To aid with additional support.

venue A place or location for an event to occur.

FOR MORE INFORMATION

Australian Centre for the Moving Image
Federation Square
Flinders Street
Melbourne, Victoria, Australia
(03) 8663 2211
Web site: http://www.acmi.net.au
This museum is all about the moving image. It educates the public about cinema, television, computer games, and the screen-based art of the future. It provided a machinima film festival showcase in 2006 and supports this medium as an art form.

Computer Graphics Society
Aldgate Valley Road
Mylor, SA 5153
Australia
E-mail: info@cgsociety.org
Web site: http://www.cgsociety.org
A global organization, CGS supports "artists at every level by offering a range of services to connect, inform, educate, and promote by celebrating achievement, excellence, and innovation in all aspects of digital art."

Museum of the Moving Image
35 Avenue at 36 Street
Astoria, NY 11106
(718) 784-0077
Web site: http://www.movingimage.us/site/site.php
This museum celebrates the moving image by educating

the public about the art, history, technique, and technology of film, television, and digital media. It hosted the 2006 Academy of Machinima Arts & Sciences award show in 2006. It supports this medium as an art form.

Web sites

Due to the changing nature of Internet links, the Rosen Publishing Group, Inc., has developed an online list of Web sites related to the subject of this book. This site is updated regularly. Please use this link to access the list:

http://www.rosenlinks.com/dcb/mach

FOR FURTHER READING

Baron, Cynthia L. *Designing a Digital Portfolio*. Indianapolis, IN: New Riders, 2003.

Busby, Jason, Zak Parrish, and Joel VanEenwyk. *Mastering Unreal Technology: The Art of Level Design*. Indianapolis, IN: Sams, 2004.

Hancock, Hugh, and Johnnie Ingram. *Machinima for Dummies*. Hoboken, NJ: John Wiley & Sons, Inc., 2007.

Hawkins, Brian. *Real-Time Cinematography for Games (Game Development Series)*. Boston, MA: Charles River Media, 2005.

Marino, Paul. *3-D Game-Based Filmmaking: The Art of Machinima*. Scottsdale, AZ: Paraglyph Press, 2004.

Marx, Christy. *Writing for Animation, Comics, and Games*. Woburn, MA: Focal Press, 2006.

Morris, Dave, Matt Kelland, and Dave Lloyd. *Machinima: Making Animated Movies in 3-D Virtual Environments*. East Sussex, UK: Ilex Press, 2005.

Roosendaal, Ton, and Carsten Wartmann. *The Official Blender GameKit: Interactive 3-D for Artists*. San Francisco, CA: No Starch Press, 2003.

Rush, Alice, and Bryan Stratton. *Paid to Play: An Insider's Guide to Video Game Careers*. New York, NY: Random House Information Group, 2006.

BIBLIOGRAPHY

Academy of Machinima Arts & Sciences. "What is Machinima?" Retrieved June 1, 2007 (http://www. machinima.org/machinima-faq.html).

Captain, Seán. "Machinima Awards Go Virtual." *Wired* magazine. Retrieved June 1, 2007 (http://www. wired.com/culture/lifestyle/news/2006/11/72062).

Marino, Paul. *3D Game-Based Filmmaking: The Art of Machinima*. Scottsdale, AZ: Paraglyph Press, 2004.

Matlack, Carol. "Video Games Go to the Movies." BusinessWeek. Retrieved June 1, 2007 (http://www. businessweek.com/technology/content/dec2005/ tc20051208_639203.htm).

Slagle, Matt. "Poll: 4 in 10 Americans Play Video Games." The Washington Post. Retrieved June 1, 2007 (http:// www.washingtonpost.com/wpdyn/content/article/ 2006/05/07/AR2006050700172_pf.html).

Strikland, Jonathan. "How Machinima Works." HowStuffWorks. Retrieved June 1, 2007 (http:// entertainment.howstuffworks.com/machinima.htm).

US Department of Labor. "Computer Software Engineers." Occupational Handbook. Retrieved June 1, 2007 (http://www.bls.gov/oco/ocos267.htm).

Walker Art Center. "Quake! Doom! Sims!" Retrieved June 1, 2007 (http://www.walkerart.org/archive/7/ A5736D3C789330FC6164.htm).

INDEX

About the Author

Holly Cefrey is an award-winning children's book author. Through her customized degree from New York University's Gallatin School, she was able to take digital arts and computer science classes from the various colleges at NYU. Cefrey has programmed very simple routines in C++ through coursework. She utilizes applications such as Director, Photoshop, ImageReady, Fireworks, and Flash to make short films and online graphics. She now designs Web sites for friends and freelance clients in her spare time.

Photo Credits

Cover and p. 1 (montage clockwise from top left) © www.istockphoto.com/Andrey Prokhorov, © www.istockphoto.com/DSGpro, © www.istockphoto.com/Antonis Papantoniou, © www.istockphoto.com/Andrzej Burak, © www.istockphoto.com/Lisa Thornberg, © www.istockphoto.com/Milan Zeremski; p. 4 © Mike Fox/ZUMA Press; pp. 8, 11 (bottom), 27 (bottom), 45 © AP Images; p. 13 © Hillsman S. Jackson; p. 16 (bottom) © Scoopt/Getty Images; p. 22 (top) © Rooster Teeth Productions, LLC; pp. 22 (bottom), 29, 32 © Getty Images; p. 25 © www.istockphoto.com/René Mansi; p. 36 © www.istockphoto.com/Andreea Manciu; p. 39 © www.mediamatic.net; p. 41 Courtesy Everett Collection; p. 47 © www.istockphoto.com/Russell Tate; p. 49 © WireImage/Getty Images; p. 50 © Strange Company 2003–2005; p. 51 © AFP/Getty Images.

Designer: Nelson Sá; **Editor:** Nicholas Croce
Photo Researcher: Cindy Reiman